The
Purple Puppy

The
Purple Puppy

...and other stories

Dill Wright

FIRST EDITION

978-1-80227-590-2 (eBook)
978-1-80227-589-6 (paperback)

*This book is dedicated to
my family... both two and four legged,
past present and future*

Contents

The Purple Puppy

"Please, Mum. Please can I paint my room purple?" said nine-year-old Alice for the fifteenth time that day. "Pleeeaaaaasseee."

"Really, Alice?" asked Alice's long-suffering mum, Rose. "It was only last week you wanted pineapple wallpaper, and before that, unicorns." She sighed. "It's not a 'no,' just a 'not yet.' Let's wait and see if you still want it in, say, a day or two from now, before we go to all that effort and expense, shall we?"

"But you know I love purple … I've always loved purple … You said when I was little I asked for a purple puppy... so you know I won't change my mind this time. Please,

Mum. Pleeeaaaaaasseee." begged Alice once again.

"Sleep now," Alice's mum said, "and we will talk about it some more tomorrow."

"Night, Mum," said Alice.

"Night, Alice, see you in the morning," said Rose, turning out the bedroom light.

Alice waited until the sound of her mum's footsteps faded into the distance before she slowly climbed out of bed and reached for her torch. By the light of her torch, Alice made her way to her desk and rummaged through her paint collection. Carefully, she selected every purple-coloured paint she could find, along with her biggest paintbrush and put them under her bed. One way or another, Alice was determined to get her purple bedroom.

With a smile on her face, Alice slipped back into bed and switched off her torch.

"Seriously, Mum, it would have been cheaper to have bought a puppy at this rate," sighed Alice's mum as she spoke to Alice's nan over a cup of tea the next day.

"Well, is it such a bad idea? Maybe a puppy is just what you all need right now. Who knows, maybe it will even stop Alice from wanting to redecorate her room every five minutes. It will be good for her to think of someone else first and take on a little responsibility."

"Hm. I suppose you could be right, as long as she doesn't decide she'd rather have a kitten next week!" said Alice's mum.

"It was meant to be," said Alice's nan, Milly, to Alice's mum the next afternoon.

"Fate and all that."

"Mmm," replied Alice's mum unbelievingly. "So, let's get this straight, somebody just happened to ask you if you wanted a puppy the day after we talked about it? Really, Mum, really?"

"Yes, I told you!" sighed Milly. "Mrs Roberts at the Post Office knows somebody who works with somebody who told somebody that their son-in-law has just had a litter of puppies and has found homes for them all except one. But we've got to be quick as they are going to put an ad in the paper at the weekend."

"Hold your horses, Mum. What sort of dog is it? How old is it? Has it had any of its jabs yet? There's lots to do and get and find out first," Rose muttered.

"Please, Rose ... pleeaase!" pleaded Milly. "There's not much time."

"It's not a 'no,' just a 'not yet.'" said Rose.

"Oh, hogwash!" exclaimed Milly, rolling her eyes. "Be spontaneous for once in your life, Rose. It's a puppy, for goodness' sake ... feed it, love it, walk it, and I will help any way I can. Now, come on, I've arranged a viewing."

"Hi, Gran," said Theo, Alice's little brother, at the school gates the following day. "Where's Mum?"

"She had to do something else right now, Theo, but don't worry, everything is fine, and all will be revealed soon," answered Milly mysteriously. "Now, where is that sister of yours?"

Twenty minutes later, Alice is skipping down the road with her brother and nan ...

"It's my room, isn't it? Mum is painting it purple right now, and that's why she didn't pick us up from school today."

"I've told you Alice, my lips are sealed. Besides, we are almost home now," replied Milly patiently.

"Just a little clue, Nan? I won't tell Mum you told us," cajoled Alice.

"No, but I will," said Theo seriously. "You can't break a promise, and you can't tell a secret … it's the rules," added Theo. "Right, Nan?"

"Well, they are not really rules, more of a good behaviour code, but you are right, Theo. We mustn't ruin your Mum's surprise … and look, here we are," said Milly opening the garden gate. "Home sweet home."

With that, Alice raced up the path with Theo hot on her heels - shedding coats, lunch boxes and book bags along the way.

"Mum? Mum, where are you?" chorused Alice and Theo excitedly.

"Err, I'm up here, in Alice's room," Rose called back down.

"See, see, I told you!" Alice squealed, making for the stairs. "She has painted my bedroom purple!"

The sight that greeted them upon entering Alice's room left Alice speechless for once. There was purple paint alright ... but not on the walls as expected. It was, however, on the bed ... the floor ... the furniture ... even on Rose!

"Technically, I didn't paint your room, Alice, ... HE did."

They all followed Rose's gaze towards the little bundle of purple fur that was leaving tiny purple paw prints over the carpet.

"Oh!" said Alice, as she spotted her purple paint supply poking out from under her bed. "Um ... Well I did always say I wanted a purple puppy ..." said Alice sheepishly.

Despite the mess, Theo was soon rolling around the bedroom floor with a very happy puppy climbing all over him and licking his face. "I can't believe we've got a puppy! What shall we call him or her?" he said.

"It's a he," answered Rose. "We can decide on a name together."

"No need," replied Alice. "He's called Periwinkle," she said, holding up a paint pot. "It's what it says on the tin."

"Mmm, Periwinkle, it suits him," chimed Milly, and so it was decided.

P	U	R	P	L	E	B	M	S	C
I	N	Q	U	T	S	V	E	L	H
N	I	W	P	O	N	Y	X	E	O
E	C	V	P	A	R	T	Y	E	C
A	O	P	Y	O	Z	M	N	P	O
P	R	I	L	F	A	C	E	O	L
P	N	Z	D	U	T	O	I	V	A
L	P	Z	E	T	V	W	O	E	T
E	D	A	N	C	I	N	G	R	E
S	T	O	M	B	P	R	W	L	V

PURPLE   PARTY

PINEAPPLE   SLEEPOVER

PUPPY   CHOCOLATE

UNICORN   DANCING

PONY   PIZZA

Just Theo

"It's not that funny, Theo," said Rose, laughing a little herself.

Theo was one of life's gigglers, and his laughs were of the infectious kind.

"Pooh, ha ha ha, winkle, ha ha ha!" he continued.

"Yes, yes, Theo, we have a CockaPOOH, and his name is PeriWINKLE, very funny. Now, are you going to get dressed today?" sighed Rose.

"Dressed?" asked Theo incredulously, picking himself up off the floor, where he'd fallen off the sofa laughing, and drew himself up to his full height of four-foot-nothing. "Dressed?" he repeated." I will have you know that this is a rebel guard uniform, and it needs to be treated with respect!"

"My mistake, Theo, and my apologies. Your mission to overthrow the Emperor and restore democracy to the galaxy is a noble one, but please put my fruit bowl back when you've finished using it as a helmet!" replied Rose with a wink.

"The force is strong with you, young Padawinkle," said Theo later that day to Periwinkle, the latest member of the family, to which Periwinkle started chewing the end of Theo's lightsaber. "I bet Qui-Gon Jinn never had this problem with Obi-Wan Kenobi," Theo sighed.

"Time to go to the party. Are you ready Theo?" asked Rose, walking into the room.

"Is Alice coming?" asked Theo.

"No, Nan's coming over to sit with her and Periwinkle, which reminds me, she said she has something for him. In fact, that's her now. Get the door, Theo, will you please? Rose asked.

"Perfect timing, Mum," said Rose, as Milly walked in. "We are just about to head off now. Are you sure you don't mind looking after them while we are gone?

"Of course not; it's my pleasure. Besides, I have a little something I knitted for the little one. Now let's see if it fits."

Milly produced a Yoda costume from her bag, much to Theo's delight.

"Give us a hand, Theo, and we can try it on him," Nan said, smiling.

A few minutes later, hands on hips, she admired her handiwork. "Perfect," she huffed.

"Nan, Yo-da best!" said Theo, cracking up at his own joke.

"And on that note ... we are off. See you in a couple of hours, but ring if you need anything, I've got my phone on me," Rose said, shutting the door behind them.

"They've got no faith in us, Periwinkle," said Milly, who promptly yawned, closed her eyes and fell fast asleep.

A few hours later, Rose and Theo returned from the party to find the entire contents of the laundry basket scattered throughout the entire downstairs. The culprit was asleep on Milly's lap, with his head on Rose's favourite bra.

"Great babysitter you turned out to be Mum," Rose muttered under her breath. "Theo, could you give us a hand to tidy this up, please? I'll go grab a basket."

On her return, Rose stopped and was treated by the amusing sight of Milly, complete with her bra on her head.

"Look, Mum, it's Princess Leia!" giggled Theo.

Rose couldn't help but laugh too. "It's not funny, Theo!" she choked out between laughs. "It's just your contagious laugh, that's all."

Just at that moment, Milly woke up, yawned, stretched and said, "I just had the strangest dream."

Theo's Favourite Star Wars Jokes

Q - How do Ewoks contact each other?

A - Ewokie-Talkies.

Q - What do you call Chewbacca when he has chocolate in his hair?

A - Chocolate chip wookie.

Knock knock.

Who's there?

Art.

Art who?

R2D2

Q - What did the dinner lady say to Luke Skywalker?

A - Use the forks, Luke.

Q - What do you call a Spanish Jedi?

A - Obi-Juan-Kenobi

Milly May

As grans go, Milly May was rather cool. Alice was always told she was the spitting image of her nan, both in looks and personality. Both took healthy interests in a whole range of activities. Alice's in the form of clubs and hobbies, of which there have been many, and Milly's in the form of evening classes, of which there have been many, many more.

There's been knitting and baking and flower arranging. Spanish lessons with the handsome Jorge. Even salsa dancing with Señor Santi. Napkin folding, origami and a book club.

This leads us to our current class of choice, pottery ... of which the Todd household was now the proud owners of six weeks' worth of... ugly... interesting...unique... different pieces of clay, or as Nan calls it, "art."

"Hello!" called out Milly, letting herself in the front door. "Anyone home? It's only me."

"Hi, Nan," replied Alice. "We are in the kitchen."

"I just brought you round this vase I made last night at pottery class. It's going really well, and Janet - that's the teacher, you know - says I have a real talent. So I brought you round my latest piece to add to the collection," said Milly. She pulled out an odd-shaped item from her rather large bag whilst at the same time looking around for the other items she'd been bringing over at regular intervals over the last six weeks. "I'll just put it with the others ... if you point me in the right direction ..."

"Oh, um, well ..." began Rose.

"It's just we ..." started Theo.

"...Haven't got anywhere to display them properly yet, Nan," jumped in Alice, saving the day before Theo could finish his sentence, which would have involved the blunt truth that they were hidden away in a cupboard where no one could see them!

"Oh, bless your hearts," said Milly, "but it just so happens I start woodworking next week. I have just decided I am going to make you all a wooden display shelf, and then you will be able to see them every day."

"Oh, Mum. That's really not necessary," protested Rose.

"It's no trouble," said Milly. "You can thank me with a cup of tea, though. Put the kettle on Rose," added Milly, pulling up a chair.

"There," said Milly, with one last thump of the hammer. "All finished." She stood back to admire her handiwork. "Now, pass me my pottery pieces Rose. I will arrange them. Julie, the flower arranging teacher, said I have an eye for it."

"That's lovely, Mum," Rose said ten minutes later. "But you shouldn't have, really."

"Nonsense! I know how much you all love my artwork."

Alice could hardly contain herself and was stifling her giggles behind her book.

Just at that moment, Theo entered the room. He closed the door behind him with a small bang, not enough for the house to shake but just enough for the newly-erected shelf to fall, breaking every item on it in the process!

For a minute, there was total silence as they all looked at each other, mouths open in total shock.

"Oh, Mum, I'm so sorry!" gasped Rose, recovering first. "All your hard work." Rose felt guilt at her relief of not having her Mum's pottery on display anymore.

However, this was short-lived by Milly's next words.

"It's okay, dears. I start painting classes next week and guess what? It's live drawing, and it can take pride of place and hang where the shelf was."

Milly May's
Mega Mixtape

Elvis Presley - Suspicious Minds

Bryan Adams - Summer of '69

Bee Jews - Jive Talking

ABBA - Dancing Queen

Boney M - Rivers of Babylon

Mamas and the Papas - California Dreamin'

George Michael - Faith

Simon and Garfunkel - Mrs Robinson

The Beatles - I Wanna Hold Your Hand

 Blondie - Call Me

Dolly Parton and Kenny Rogers - Islands in the Stream

Queen - I Want to Break Free

Rose's Relaxing Retreat

"But Mum, it's too much, and besides, I can't just go and leave you all," protested Rose.

"Nonsense. You deserve it and it's only for one night. I'm sure we can manage without you for that long, can't we, kids?" Milly replied, looking from Alice to Theo.

"What about Periwinkle? He's a handful at the moment, into everything, and you can't take your eyes off of him for more than a few minutes ..." added Rose.

"We can imagine, Rose. Just you go and enjoy yourself," said Milly.

"We've got this, Mum," chimed in Alice.

"Well, if you are all sure," said Rose, not at all sounding sure herself. "I'd better go and pack then."

An hour later, Rose found herself checking into a beautiful hotel and spa. It was home for the next 24 hours, and she slowly felt her doubts and worries fade.

She quickly located her room and, after wheeling her suitcase in, she collapsed onto the bed. Rose felt a moment of guilt at doubting her family could manage without her. But really, it was only a moment as the next thing Rose knew, her suitcase barked and toppled over. Quickly, Rose unzipped the case and came face to face with a very excited Periwinkle.

"He's got to be here somewhere. Everybody look again! Theo, you take the garden, Alice, you look upstairs, and I will search down here. Dogs don't just vanish into thin air!"

They all met up again 15 minutes later in the kitchen.

"Are we going to ring Mum and tell her we lost Peri?" asked Theo.

"She is going to kill us!" added Alice. "She said we couldn't be trusted, and look, we just proved her right ... and I HATE proving Mum right!"

"Now, now, children, no need to panic just yet. He hasn't been gone that long. I'm sure he's just off exploring somewhere, and he'll be home as soon as he feels hungry. No need to tell your mum just yet. After all, the whole point of this trip was for her to relax and besides... I also hate proving your mum right, too," said Milly, pulling a face. "Now, who's up for a game of cards?"

"How did you manage to get in there?" Rose asked Periwinkle at about the same time as the big search. "All I can think is that you must have climbed in whilst I was packing, snuggled under some clothes and fell asleep there. Oh my, I wonder if they've noticed you've gone yet? If so, they must be out of their minds with worry. I better give them a call!" And with that, Rose reached for her phone.

"Hi, Mum, is that you?" asked Rose a moment later.

"Hi, Rose," replied Milly. "What are you

doing ringing us? You are supposed to be relaxing and not worrying. We are all fine here." Added Milly.

"Are you sure, Mum?" asked Rose. "All of you are okay? Even Periwinkle?"

"Yes, yes, I told you, we are having a great time, nothing to worry about here! Now, I better go; we are playing cards, and you know how Alice cheats if you turn your back for one minute. You just enjoy yourself, and we will see you tomorrow. Bye, love."

And with that, Milly hung up the phone and left Rose listening to silence and a panting Periwinkle. "Something tells me they know you are missing but either didn't want me to worry or just didn't want me to know!" Rose said to Periwinkle, filling one of the complimentary saucers with water for a thirsty Periwinkle. "And I think it's the latter, Peri. Well, two can play at that game," mused Rose.

"Was that Mum?" asked Alice and Theo in unison. "What did she say? Did you tell her about Periwinkle?" they chorused when Milly returned.

"Yes and no, in that order." Replied Milly. "I just couldn't bring myself to tell her. We just need to hope and pray he turns up before your mum gets back. Now, who's hungry? I'm ready for my dinner, I am. All this fuss has given me quite an appetite." Milly started opening the kitchen cupboard doors in search of a meal and a distraction.

"One for you," said Rose, giving Periwinkle a strawberry courtesy of room service the next morning. "And one for me," she finished, popping the last strawberry into her mouth. Both were wrapped up in the health spa's fluffy white towels and robe after sharing a luxurious bubble bath together. "This is the life, Peri," Rose said, stretching out across the enormous bed. To which Peri yipped in agreement. "But I suppose all good things must come to an end - or so they say." With a big sigh, Rose rose from the bed and began preparations to leave.

"Right, kids, let's get our stories straight," said Milly at about the same time Rose and Periwinkle were enjoying their breakfast. "If there's still no sign of Periwinkle by the time your mum gets home, we will tell her he has been with us this whole time but that he must have got out as she arrived back. Then we can search in earnest. We can make and put up posters and form a proper search party."

"But what if we never see Peri again?" sobbed Theo. "He's my best friend."

"Don't you worry, my dear. We will soon have your best friend home safe and sound," Milly said, giving Theo a big hug.

"I'm afraid you are going to have to get back in, Peri," said Rose, looking from

Periwinkle to the open suitcase and back again. "Just until we get to the car."

As if Periwinkle understood, he stepped into the suitcase and promptly curled up and fell asleep.

Once in the car, Rose unzipped the suitcase, but Peri chose to stay in his new 'bed' amongst Rose's clothes and stayed there the whole way home.

"Right, just one last time, Peri," said Rose, zipping the case back up. "Just until we get you inside."

Rose managed to slip into the house unnoticed. She carefully wheeled the suitcase into the living room, unzipped it and went in search of her family. They were in the kitchen making her her favourite chocolate cake (almost as if they were trying to get into her good books or something).

"Mum, you're home!" shouted Alice and Theo, throwing themselves at her.

"I missed you all so much!" said Rose, hugging them all back.

At that moment, Periwinkle came bounding into the kitchen.

"How have you all been? How was Periwinkle? I hope he behaved," asked Rose, holding back a smile.

"He was so good; you wouldn't have even known he was here," answered Milly, with a wink at Alice and Theo.

Rose's Chocolate Cake Recipe

INGREDIENTS:

For the cake:

200g golden caster sugar
200g unsalted butter
4 large eggs
200g self-raising flour
2 tbsp cocoa powder
1 tsp baking powder
1/2 tsp vanilla extract
2 tbsp milk

For the buttercream:

100g milk chocolate
200g butter
400g icing sugar
5 tbsp cocoa powder
2 tbsp milk

METHOD:

Heat oven to gas mark 5. Butter two 20cm sandwich tins and line with baking paper.

Beat together all of the cake ingredients in a large mixing bowl.

Divide the mixture between the two tins. Bake for 20 minutes or until cooked.

Leave to cool, then turn out onto a wire rack until completely cooled.

For the buttercream, melt the chocolate stirring every 30 seconds. Allow to cool for 5 minutes.

Mix the butter and icing sugar together.

Sift in the cocoa powder, add the melted chocolate and milk and mix until smooth.

Sandwich the cakes together with half of the buttercream and spread the second half on the top.

Periwinkle's Pack

Hi, my name is Periwinkle, or Peri or Winkle or Peri-Peri, depending on which member of my pack is calling me and also depending on what I've done, apparently.

Anyway, I recently found my pack, and I just wanted to introduce you to them, and me, for that matter.

As it turns out, I don't really look like the rest of my pack or sound like them, and if I'm totally honest, I don't always know what they are saying. It's as if they are speaking a different language to me sometimes. But I'm learning, and these are some of the words I do know.

Sit. This involves me having to put my bum on the floor. I'm not quite sure why I have to do this. Maybe they think I look tired or something, but I don't mind, really, as I usually then get a pat on the head and a treat.

Lay down. This one means I have to be completely flat on the floor. Again I'm not too sure why I have to do this, perhaps something is above me, and I need to avoid it. Still, it's not a problem for me because I get more praise and treats.

Dinner. Now, this is a good one, possibly my favourite. It means go to the kitchen and there they will put a pile of food out, just for me. This is different from the rest of the pack's dinner, where I wait under the table and Theo drops things for me. Usually,

I don't like these things so much, but Theo always seems very happy with me.

Bath. Not so keen on this one. It involves me getting very wet and soapy, and I smell really bad afterwards, but it makes Rose very happy.

Walk. Another good one, unless the bathwater is being showered on me. I think my pack call this rain.

Good Boy. This is a very good one, where I get lots of cuddles and treats. Maybe it's because it's two words?

Now I would like to introduce you to my pack. First, there is Theo, he's my best friend, and we play together A LOT. Next, there's Alice. She's the bossy one; it's always … "Sit, Peri … Stay, Peri … Paw, Peri … Peri, Peri, Peri." Oh, and another thing, Alice does

NOT share food.

Next is Rose. She tells me off a lot ... especially if I dig in the garden. I don't know why I'm not allowed to when she is; however, as she is usually the one that gives me dinner, I will let her off. Then there is Milly, a part-time pack member. She doesn't sleep here with us at night, but she often sleeps here with me during the day. I think when she is not here, she is out foraging because when she returns, she brings treats, toys and clothes, usually for me. For some reason, Rose doesn't tell me off whenever I chew something Milly brings. It's very confusing.

Anyway, that's my pack. I love them, and they love me. I think they call it "family."

Made in United States
North Haven, CT
20 December 2022

29686148R00037